MANY CHILDREN

Religions Around the World

By

M. Angele Thomas, Ed.D.

and

Mary L. Ramey

Cover Photo by
R. Crawford Nace

Illustrations by
Patti L. Lucas

Published by M. Angele Thomas
Reston, VA

First Edition

Printed in the United States of America

Library of Congress Catalog Card Number: 87-91771

Library of Congress Cataloging in Publication Data
Thomas, M. Angele
Many Children—Religions Around the World
Includes Glossary and Index

Summary: Early-level introduction to origins of religions of India, Asia, North Africa, Israel, Europe and America.

ISBN 0-9619293-0-8

Table of Contents

Dedicated to
Talitha, Jeremiah and
all their friends

Preface

"Who is God? What is God? Is God a man or woman?" What parent or teacher has not been asked these and many other questions? The authors, one a parent—one a teacher, have been surrounded by the curiosity of children. It is because of our desire to help boys and girls come to understand what God means to a variety of people that this book was written.

No bias is intended toward any religion. Rather, a healthy respect and value for each individual's belief in a Supreme Being is our single-minded purpose. The philosophy of Ugo Betti is our creed: Every person is like a tiny drop of water without which the whole world would thirst.

If children are motivated by this work to search for truth and to achieve peace in their lives, then we will be amply gratified. We thank Paul A. Dooley, a long-standing scholar of comparative religions for his review and constructive comments on the manuscript. The interpretations in this book are solely those of the authors.

Who is God? We are told: "A little child shall lead them."[1] We welcome their thoughts.

M. Angele Thomas, Ed.D.

Mary L. Ramey

[1]Isaiah 11:6 (King James Version)

TIME LINE

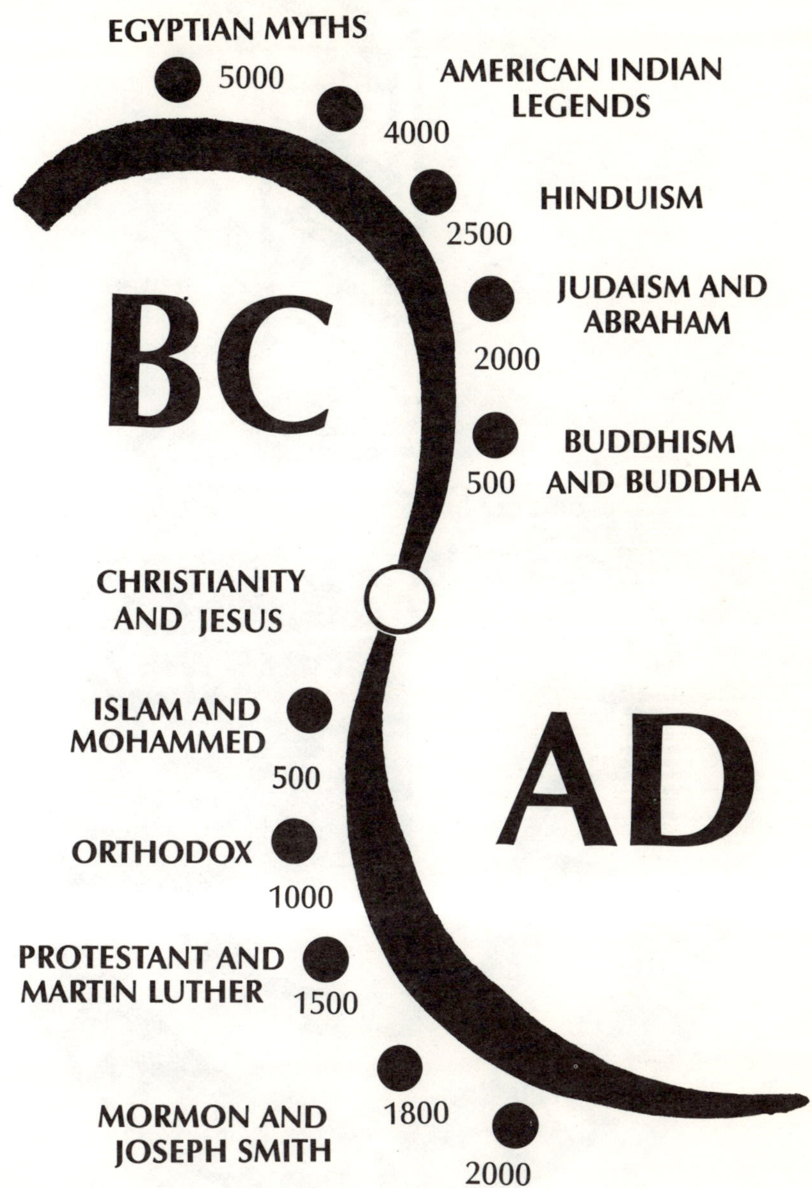
EGYPTIAN MYTHS
5000
AMERICAN INDIAN LEGENDS
4000
HINDUISM
2500
JUDAISM AND ABRAHAM
2000
BUDDHISM AND BUDDHA
500
BC
CHRISTIANITY AND JESUS
ISLAM AND MOHAMMED
500
AD
ORTHODOX
1000
PROTESTANT AND MARTIN LUTHER
1500
MORMON AND JOSEPH SMITH
1800
2000

Egyptian goddess of truth

Children of Egypt

When we talk about Egyptians and their religion, we are talking about really old and ancient people. They lived about 5,000 years ago in the land of Egypt. No one really knows for certain when the religion began. Back then people didn't know what made sunshine, night time, the moon and the stars. In trying to figure everything out, different people came up with different ideas.

Myths

They told these ideas to their children. These ideas or stories were called myths (sounds like with). The stories were passed down year after year in tradition. The Egyptians also wrote down many of their ideas in a special picture writing on beautiful paper called papyrus. They also carved and painted stories in pictures on walls of their buildings. No one could ever prove that these myths were true. Sometimes the myths changed whenever a person came up with a new idea.

This is like the four blind children in the fable who are touching different parts of an elephant. One girl puts her arms around the elephant's big leg and says this animal must look like a tree. A boy reaches up and pats its side. He thinks the elephant is shaped like a wall. A second girl grabs hold of the elephant's trunk and says that it feels like a snake. Another boy holds onto the tail. "You are all wrong," he says. "This animal is tiny like a rope." Were any of these children's ideas right? Can you see how they came up with different ideas?

Many people all over the world had myths. The Egyptian myths were part of the Egyptian religion. The Egyptians lived in North Africa near a huge river named the Nile. This river had wonderful dirt along its banks for growing crops. The Egyptians knew they couldn't make the water or earth or trees or rocks. They decided that there must be something greater than men who could do these things. They decided powerful beings must have made all the things in the world. The Egyptians called these beings "gods."

Egyptian scale of justice with the heart and feather of truth

Sacrifice

They wanted the gods to help them grow food to eat each year and to give them water and good weather. They made statues out of stone to look like the gods. They built great churches called temples and prayed to the gods for all the people. They brought some of the food they grew and gave it to the priests and the gods in temples. This is called a sacrifice.

Egyptian Gods

The ancient Egyptians were also amazed at birds which could fly up higher than men could reach. They were amazed at the animals that could run faster and carry heavier loads than men. They thought that the animals and birds had strength and power because they were gods.

Children in Egypt learned to think of the animals as gods. They were taught to pray to them. When animals died, they were buried in special cemeteries with fancy tombstones. They thought the crocodile in the river was a god. If a child fell into the river and was eaten by a crocodile, everyone would cry for the child. But they would also be proud because they believed that the crocodile god had especially chosen the child to go live with the other gods.

Have you ever seen a picture of a part-person, part-animal? Since the animals were so strong and men were so smart, the Egyptians thought that the gods must be part animal and part man. That is how they drew them in their pictures and carved them in their statues. There were men gods and women goddesses for everything. There were gods for rain and fire, earth and water, happiness and sadness. The kings of Egypt were called pharaohs. Everybody thought the gods gave the pharaohs great powers, so the people called the pharaohs gods, too. The people told about all the wonderful things their kings and gods did. They would sing songs and tell stories to their children.

One story goes that Horus was a powerful sky god. He took the shape of a falcon bird. Egyptians thought that the sun was his right eye and the moon his left eye. The sun had many names. Children called it one thing when it was coming up in the morning and another name when it was going down at night. The moon was supposed to be the sun's brother. Another myth said that the sky was a goddess or female god. She was a cow standing over the earth. Her stomach was supposed to be the sky. Some Egyptians thought the stars were born every morning and then swallowed up every night by a pig god.

Pyramids

Have you ever seen pictures of the pyramid buildings of old Egypt? These were huge graves for important people who had died.

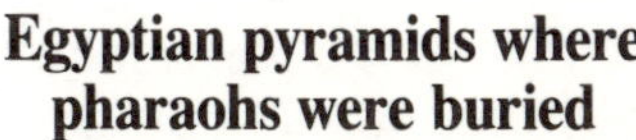

Egyptian pyramids where pharaohs were buried

When people died, the ancient Egyptians believed that they went on a long journey and took all their things with them to live in the Underworld. This was the Egyptian idea for heaven. The Egyptians put everything in the grave with the dead person that he or she would need on the journey. They buried food and wine and sometimes seeds. People watered the seeds so they would grow new food for the person to eat on his trip. Funerals might last for seven days. They washed the person's body in the Nile River and cleaned it out. Then they wrapped it round and round with linen material and plastered it until it was hard. These wrapped bodies were called mummies. Sometimes the mummies were decorated with jewels and painted to look like the person. You can still see a mummy in a museum.

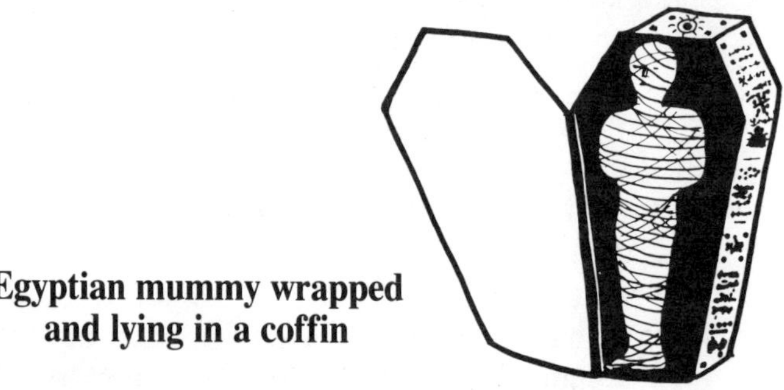

Egyptian mummy wrapped and lying in a coffin

The mummy was put into a wooden box called a coffin. Then it was taken in a long parade to the cemetery to be buried. The kings and rich people were put into huge tombs shaped like pyramids. The fancy ones were like palaces with furniture inside, and paintings and statues of their servants. Then the pyramid was shut up tight with a secret door so that no one could come in and bother it.

Children in old Egypt might ask, "Will all people go to the underworld when they die?" Their parents would tell them this: "The gods in the next world will judge each person by a scale. On one side of the scale will sit the person's heart for all the good things that she or he has done. On the other side of the scale will sit an ostrich feather for the sign of truth. If the heart and the truth feather weigh the same the person will be judged a good person and he will be allowed to finish his journey to a happy underworld."

What if the scale tipped the other way? The Egyptians believed that if the gods found the person to be bad, he or she would be destroyed by a monster in the underworld.

There are not very many people in the world who still believe in the Egyptian myths. Yet the Egyptian religion gave us some very interesting ideas. From the Egyptians we learned picture writing called "hieroglyphics." We also learned that the Egyptians believed that life did not just end when a person died. They believed in a happy life forever. Their special sign was a cross with a loop on the top. It means "eternal life."

The Egyptian sign for eternal life

Children of Hinduism

One of the oldest religions that people know about comes from the country of India about 2,500 years before Jesus Christ was born. It wasn't started by any one person. People who practiced this religion had many different ideas about who made them and where they came from. They had many ideas about heaven and life after we died here on earth.

Some of the people that live in India are called Hindus. All Hindus don't have the same religious beliefs even though they may have the same family customs. Their way of life is called Hinduism.

Caste System

One religion in India is called Vedism. The first people that lived in India were dark-skinned. Later, a light-skinned people came. They were called Aryans. They wanted all the land that the dark-skinned people had so they made war with them. The Aryans won and ruled India. They married some of the dark-skinned people and taught them their own religion. They also wanted the dark-skinned people to be their slaves and servants so they made a strict law called the caste system (sounds like cast). Under the caste law, you could only be the same thing your parents were. If your father had been a farmer then you could only be a farmer—you could not be a businessman or a king or queen. If your father had been a soldier, then you could not be a priest or farmer. You had to be a soldier. The caste laws were so strict that you could not even be friends with someone who was not in your group of people. You could not touch them or work with them.

The four groups of people in the caste system were:

1. Priests who said prayers in the temples
2. Soldiers and rulers who made the laws

3. Businessmen who had shops and traded goods
4. Servants who did the work of cooking, cleaning and washing

Under these four groups of people was another group called the "untouchables." They were untouchable because nobody else wanted to touch them. They were poor and dirty. They never learned anything because they were not allowed to go to school. They had to do all the hard jobs like picking up garbage and cleaning barns.

Gandhi

One very famous man in India was named Gandhi. He felt sorry for the untouchables and tried to help them. Gandhi made the people of India see that the caste laws were not good laws for India. Now those laws are gone and all the people are supposed to be equal.

Hindus believe there is one great spirit in the world. They believe that the spirit lives inside each person, too. One Hindu name for God is Brahma. Hindus have churches called temples and priests who say prayers there. The priests are called Brahmins. But a Hindu man and his family do not have to go to the temples if they don't want to. Usually each family or person prays alone to this great spirit in the world whenever he or she wants to. Sometimes a Hindu will say this

Hindu temple

prayer: "God is one and infinite, the light of light." This means there is only one God. He never began and he will never end. He will show us what to do.

Wheel of Life

Hindus believe that people leave their bodies when they die. Then their family burns the body until it turns to ashes. Hindus feel it is all right to burn the body because the body is no longer important. Hindus believe that they will be born again into a new body with new parents. This idea is called the Hindu "Wheel of Life." Believing that people are born over and over again after they die is called "reincarnation."

Being born again in the Hindu Wheel of Life

What must Hindu children do in their religion? They try to obey all the rules of their religion, say all the prayers, love God and be kind to other people. Then they believe they will receive the reward of being born into a new and better life. If they have not learned to be good, Hindus think that they may be born into an unhappy, hard life. Some Hindus are afraid that they might even by born again as an animal or insect.

That is why Hindu boys and girls do not like to hurt any living thing like a bird or dog or another person. They do not like to kill animals for food. Some Hindu children do not even like to step on insects. They are taught to be gentle and respect all life. A Hindu will not kill a cow to eat its beef because a cow is a holy animal in India. The cow reminds Hindus that they are brothers with all things, even with animals like cows. They must take care of all the things that God has made.

Karma

Hindu parents teach their children: “Be good to others and they will be good to you.” There is a reward for being good. There is a punishment for being bad. This is called “karma.” Hindus must be careful of what they do in their life so they will have a good karma. They believe a good karma will be the reward of being born again into a better life. Someday, if their karma gets better and better, they will escape from the Wheel of Life and will be able to go to a happy place they think of as heaven. The Hindu idea of heaven is called Nirvana. Nirvana will never end. There is no hurt or pain in this place.

A happy festival for Hindu boys and girls is called Divali. It is the Hindu New Year. It comes in the fall. Girls and boys, mothers and fathers and friends everywhere give presents to each other. All the people light lamps and put them on their door posts to show their happiness.

What do Hindus wear? Sometimes the women wear brightly colored cloth of silk or cotton. They wrap it round and round for a skirt and then tuck it over their heads for a shawl. This wrap is called a sari. The men might wear white pants and shirts that are loose. Sometimes they wear a white cloth wrapped around their head. This is called a turban.

Hindu sari and turban

Hindu boys and girls learn songs and prayers from the holy book called the Vedas. They usually learn to read Sanskrit which was the written language of some Indian people.

Brahma

For Hindus, God is not just one person or being. He is all people, men or women. God is all things. If a Hindu thinks about God as a strong protector, he will give him the name "Protector" and will make a statue and build a temple to put the statue in. Then some people will come and pray to this statue to remind them that God is their protector. If a Hindu thinks God is a woman who made the whole world, he calls her "Mother" and makes a statue of her. Since Hindus have many ideas of what God is like, they use many names and faces. Sometimes this can be very confusing to people of other religions. One important name for God is Brahma. Sometimes you may see a picture of Brahma with three sides. It means there are three persons in this idea of God. If

Hindu Brahma, three persons in one

Brahma comes to earth again to visit the Hindu people, they may call him by another name and give him another face in their paintings and statues. When people write about many gods or ideas of gods, they spell it with a small "g." When they write about the one and only Supreme God who made all things, knows all things and can do all things, they write it with a capital "G." You will see these different spellings many times when you study about the religions of the world.

Hindu people are always looking for God. They are not too upset if there are troubles in the world. They believe that all things will work out in time as God planned it according to the ideas of karma.

Yoga

Boy sitting in a yoga position

Some Hindus don't care about any of the comfortable things in this world. They are more interested in learning about God and praying to him. They give up nice things like houses and their work, money and clothes. They walk around the country just being happy if someone will offer them some food to eat. These people are respected in India because they are trying to get close to God. These holy people are called yogis. Some yogis sit quietly for many hours with their legs crossed.

What are they doing? They are doing yoga. They are very still and relaxed and they listen for the voice of God inside them. Many people who are not Hindus or yogis practice yoga today just to help them feel good and healthy and peaceful.

Ganges

Probably the most important thing for Hindus to do in their religion is to make a trip to a holy river before they die. One holy river in India is called the Ganges River. The land is hot and dry. Rivers are holy or special to the people because they need water in order to live. They believe the river has power. If you were a Hindu child in India, your whole village might make a trip together to the Ganges River. You would walk up one side and down the other. At sunrise or sunset, you would say prayers to the sun. Hindus remember that God made the sun. Then you would step into the river to wash and feel God's goodness all around you. Sometimes the Hindu people go to the river when they are very old and ready to die. They want to die near the river. It helps them to leave this life in peace.

Hindu girl bathing in a holy river

Hinduism began in India. It has changed some, but it is still an important religion all over the world. You can be a Hindu if you are born to Hindu parents. Or you could study about the religion from a Hindu teacher. A new kind of Hinduism is in the United States of America. It is called Hari Krishna.

One thing Hinduism teaches us is to respect all living things. If you meet a Hindu boy from India, he might say hello by folding his hands and bowing his head. This shows that he respects you.

Children of Buddhism

Buddhism is a very old religion that started in India about 500 years before Jesus was born. Once there was a young prince named Siddhartha. He was a Hindu boy in the land of India. Siddhartha lived in a beautiful castle where there were always happiness and riches all his life. His father never let him go outside the castle so he did not know what it was like in the rest of the world. When he grew up and went outside the castle gates for the first time, he saw that there was not always happiness like he knew it. He saw poor people, suffering and sick people. He saw old people for the first time, and he saw dying people, too.

Searching for the Truth

Maybe you have wondered why people are poor or very sick or dying. So did Siddhartha. It bothered him so much. He decided he must search for the reason for all this misery.

Siddhartha decided to join the group of holy men Indians called Jains. He didn't eat much food and he made himself become hungry. He prayed a lot and spent all his time wondering about the truth in life. But he did not find any answers. He left the holy men and started to take better care of himself. Then he began to sit quietly for a long time and think only of the reason for life and death. Finally a great thought came into his mind. He thought that the reason people were unhappy in this world was because they wanted too many things that they could not have—like toys and houses and money. He thought that the way to find happiness and freedom from suffering was in each person's own mind. Each person should take care of his mind and body, because we need our minds and bodies to live our lives on this earth.

Buddha

After Siddhartha had these great thoughts, he believed he knew the truth. He started to teach about freedom from suffering called Nirvana. The people started calling him Buddha. Buddha means "a person who has learned the truth." So now the people started to follow

Statue of Buddha with hands showing sign of peace

Buddha as he walked from town to town in India. They wanted to hear the things that he was teaching about life and death. Siddhartha went back to his castle and told his family about what he had learned. They believed him and asked him to show them how to find happiness, too.

Meditation

Buddha said, "You should not believe me just because I tell you that this is true. You should sit in a quiet place like I do and make your mind very silent. The truth will come to your mind and you will know how to be happy." This quiet time for the mind is called "meditation."

But the people wanted Buddha to lead them, so he gave them these rules to help them:

1. Do not kill any living thing.
2. Do not steal or cheat.
3. Do not tell a lie.
4. Do not put hard drinks or drugs into your body.

Some people in India liked Buddha's teaching because Buddha told them that people could escape from the Wheel of Life if they did good things in this life. That means that they could become happy without having to be born again into another body. Many people joined Buddha on his walks. They decided to get together in groups so they could help each other learn about happiness and meditation. They called themselves monks or sometimes lamas. They did not work or build houses or look for food. They stayed in little huts where they sat in quiet meditation. Like the yogis, they were thankful if some kind person brought them food to eat. Later, rich people built them large buildings with many rooms so all the monks could have places to live.

When Buddha was alive, girls and women in India were not very important. A friend of Buddha's asked him, "Can women become free from suffering like men can?" Buddha said, "Yes, they can." Then the friend asked, "Buddha, so why don't you let women join our group? There are many women who believe what you teach and who want to learn about the road to happiness, too." At first Buddha did not want them to join, but finally he said, "Yes." Then the women built huts and lived and prayed together. These women were called Buddhist nuns.

Story of Ryonen

Once there was a young beautiful girl named Ryonen. She was the servant of the Queen of Japan. Ryonen wanted to join the Buddhist nuns. The leader of the nuns said that Ryonen couldn't join them because she was too pretty and soon she would be thinking about getting married. This made Ryonen sad. She knew she wanted to join the nuns and learn about the road to heaven. Ryonen had a plan. She cut her hair very short and made herself look ugly to prove to the nuns that she would not leave them someday for a husband. The nuns saw that Ryonen was really serious about her choice. They let her join their group and she was very happy.

When Buddha was alive, he walked from town to town and city to city for many years teaching the people all he knew. Kind people took him into their homes every place he went. Finally, when he was 80 years old he died. Before he died, he told his people and all the children around him, "I will not tell you what God is or what heaven is like. Each one of you is part of the spirit of the whole world. Each one of you is part of God. The world will not be happy until you make it happy. You must take care of each other. The best thing you can do in your life is to help someone who needs you." Then he died.

His friends went out into the world and told everyone about the teachings they had learned from Buddha and that is how the Buddhist religion began.

Eight Duties

Buddhist children learn the eight duties each person must do to be happy.

1. Know the truth.
2. Do things for the right reasons.
3. Speak in a kind way to other people.
4. Behave in the correct way.

5. Do the right kind of work. (Don't take a job that will hurt other people).
6. Try your best.
7. Know who you are . . . don't fool yourself.
8. Think good thoughts at meditation time.

The beautiful lotus flower with eight petals that open up is a sign of all these things. Buddha himself did not write down any of his

Lotus flower with eight open petals

teachings. After he died, his monks wrote down the things he said and did in a book called the Sutras. These make up the holy books of the Buddhist religion.

When young boys and girls turn 15, they can join the monks or nuns if they want to. Sometimes they shave the hair off their heads. They wear long cloths wrapped around their body. These cloths are

Young Buddhist monk with a prayer wheel

often bright yellow, red or orange. In some countries, Buddhist monks and nuns spin a wooden wheel on a stick. The wheel has a prayer carved on it. When it spins around, Buddhists believe their prayer goes up to heaven. Or they may have a prayer written on a beautiful flag. Each time the flag waves the prayer is said. Sometimes they ring bells. It is always a happy sound. Monks and nuns do not marry anyone or have a family. They spend their time praying and doing quiet meditation. They teach others what they have learned about life and death, about happiness and freedom from suffering.

Even though Buddhism is much like the Hindu religions in India, many Indians did not want to practice it. Hindus believed at one time that each person should stay in his own group and not speak to other groups. Buddhism did not teach that. Buddha let all people come together—men and women, black and white, rich and poor. The only people Buddha would not let into his group were the people who did bad things like steal or cheat or kill.

Shrines and Temples

When the followers of Buddha traveled all over the world and taught about Buddhism, they made statues of Buddha and built shrines to put the statues in. Sometimes you see a statue of Buddha with one hand up and one hand down. This is a sign for peace. They also built large churches where people could come together and pray. These were called temples. One of the most beautiful temples is in the country of Cambodia. This is near China.

Buddhist shrine

Now you can find Buddhism in America, too. A new kind of Buddhist teachings are called Zen. You can be a Buddhist if you are born to parents who practice Buddhism. Or you may study the life and teachings of Siddhartha the Buddha and believe in him. The greatest thing that Buddhism teaches boys and girls is to like themselves and look into their own minds when they want to know the truth.

Children of The Center
(American Indians)

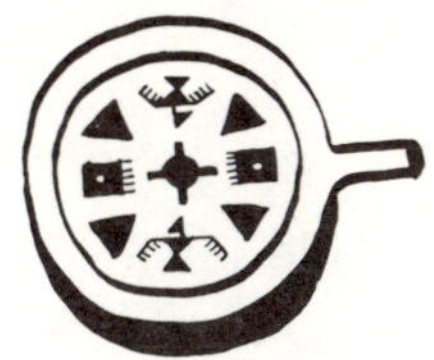

American Indian drum used for songs and prayer chants

In summer many people in America come together for a celebration. It is called the Sun Dance. It is one of the many celebrations of a people called American Indians. They often live together in groups called tribes. Native American Indians were the first people to live in America. Their religion is so very old, it is hard to tell when it began.

The Sun Dance is one of the biggest holidays. It is a very important time for American Indian boys and girls. It starts because someone in the tribe says a prayer of thanks or asks a favor from God. A small tree is cut down and set up as a pole in the middle of camp. The pole is painted and decorated. The person who says the prayer comes to the middle of the camp and all the people help. Boys and girls sing. The people sing long songs called chants and people beat the drums. It is both serious and happy.

A house of trees and logs or skins is built around the pole. This house is called a lodge and it becomes a holy place during the Sun Dance. The people of the tribe make a circle around the pole. They make the circle to show they are all friends together. Then some of the people may stop eating for a day or more. This is called fasting. American Indians think that fasting helps them to keep their body empty so their spirits can feel closer to God. It is very hot in the lodge. Sometimes they pour water over hot rocks to make steam. This helps to clean the body to make more room for the spirit.

Peace Pipe

American Indians also smoke peace pipes. Maybe you have seen

American Indian peace pipe

pictures of them. The peace pipes are made out of wood or red pipestone. The smoke from the peace pipe goes up as a prayer. The Indian blows smoke east and west, north and south. Then he blows smoke up and down. This shows love and respect for the whole world. After that, he blows smoke on himself. Now he is showing that he is joined with the whole world. It is the American Indian's way of saying, "I am part of what God made and I am in the middle of it."

During the Sun Dance, old people tell stories to young children of what happened long ago. They tell about great hunters and chiefs, about brave men and women, about bad times and good times. American Indians sometimes draw pictures on buffalo skins to mark important things that happened that year.

Tradition

They never wrote down any of their ideas of religion in holy books like other people did. American Indians kept their religion alive by telling the stories to young people. The young people grew up and told these stories again to their children. This is called tradition. Tradition was all they had for a long, long time. After the white men came to America, there was a great Cherokee chief named Sequoia. He was the first American Indian to write down the language of his tribe in a way that all people could read and write it. Then the American Indians started to write down all their traditions.

Face Painting

The Sun Dance can last for many days. The children dress in costumes made from animal skins and bird feathers. They paint their faces with a favorite design. Face painting is an important custom of American Indians. One mother in a Pawnee Indian tribe painted this design on the face of her daughter. It is her way of making a special

Pawnee Indian girl with a face painting for a blessing

prayer for her daughter. It is a half circle across the girl's face with a straight line down the girl's nose. The circle means the sky which is the home of the sky spirit Tirawa, and the center line is breath which is coming down from heaven into the girl's nose on the way to her heart. The prayer means that the mother wants all good things from heaven to come to her daughter. It is a way of showing her love. Face painting is still popular with other Americans. Have you ever gone to a fair or carnival and had someone paint a butterfly or flower on your face?

When the people come to the circle around the pole, they remember that they are made by the same God who made the sun. American Indians call God by many names—Earth Maker, Father, Man Above, Great Holy or Master of Life. They feel very close to God because they live close to the earth and all the things God made on the earth. American Indians also believe in good and bad spirits. They pray to their fathers and grandfathers who have died and gone on to live in the spirit world. This is what the American Indians think of as heaven. Sometimes they want to talk with a spirit from the spirit world. At other times, they believe that one of their fathers or grandfathers comes back to earth to be born again as a new baby.

Visions

If you were a young Indian child growing up, you might go alone to a quiet place like a mountain side or a forest or desert. Maybe you would sit alone in the sun without eating or drinking for a long time. You would try to be very quiet and brave and strong. You might pray that one of your grandfathers would come from the spirit world in a dream. This dream is called a vision.

American Indian boy praying for a vision

The dream is very important to American Indians. They believe it helps boys and girls know who they are and what they must do with their lives. When the vision is over, they go back to the people in their tribe and tell them about it. When the people hear the story of the vision, they decide if the child is going to be an important person in the tribe. American Indians think that God sends special people from time to time to help the tribe.

Medicine Man

Have you seen pictures of an American Indian medicine man? He is a shaman. The shaman has one of the most important jobs of all the people. When American Indians are sick or worried, they go to the shaman. He has medicines for sick bodies that he makes from wild plants. He also says special prayers and chants for sick spirits. He learned about these from his fathers and uncles.

Indians believe they must live in peace with all the earth. If they do not, they hurt their body, mind and spirit. The medicine man's biggest job in the tribe is to help bring back peace to the sick person.

Circle

The circle is important to American Indians. They draw it on their

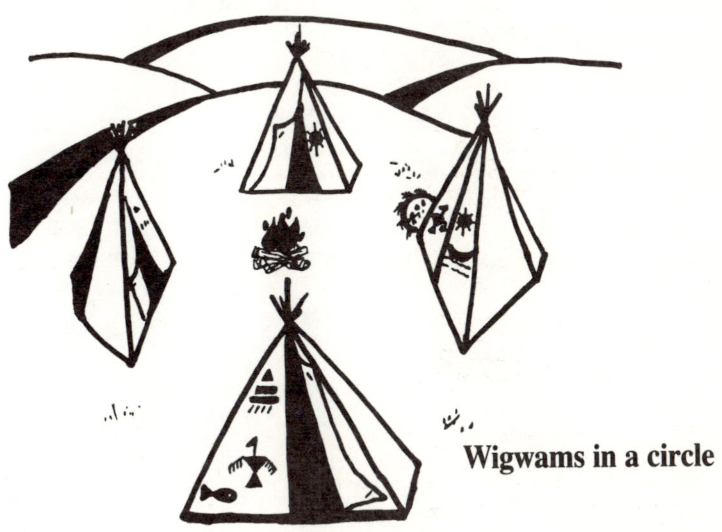

Wigwams in a circle

tents; they weave it in their rugs. They make their camps in a circle. They believe that God created everything round, like the sun and moon with the earth in the center of all of it. In a circle, the people are all together. They help and protect each other. They watch out for the children who play in the circle of tents. Indian tents are called wigwams or teepees. They keep happiness in and danger out. If one person in the tribe does something terribly wrong, it hurts all the people. That person must be punished for a while, but usually the people forgive the person if he or she tries to do better. If the people feel that the bad persons are dangerous, they are sent away and cannot live in the tribe anymore.

Do you like the green grass and the quiet coolness of the lakes and rivers? So do American Indians. Many of the stories of Indians are about nature and animals and birds. American Indians feel like brothers and sisters of the earth and sky, the animals and plants. They like to live in peace with all the world. Sometimes it is hard to live close to nature if the winter is very cold and the storms are very strong. One time there was a very great storm with much thunder and lightning. A Yuki Indian medicine man prayed this prayer:

> "Please stop. My people are afraid. Why are you doing this? Father, be careful. We're living here. Be easy with us. We are doing the best we can."

Before white people came to America, there were more than 2,000 different Indian tribes. They had different customs and spoke different languages. Sometimes they could not understand each other, so they made signs with their hands and arms to speak to each other. If they wanted to talk to someone far away, they would light a fire and let smoke signals rise up into the air. You could see them from hill to hill.

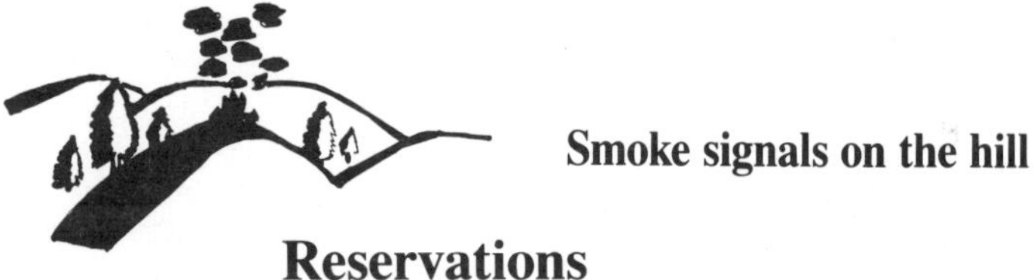

Smoke signals on the hill

Reservations

Today American Indians speak their own languages and English, also. They live in all parts of America. Some American Indians who want to live in their old ways and keep their traditions have houses on land that is saved just for Indians. This land is called a reservation. Other people are not allowed on the reservations without permission from the tribe. When the American Indians have great holy days like the Sun Dance, they share it with everyone who wants to come and watch. They are proud to show other people their traditions and their religion. Perhaps someday you may be invited to see a Sun Dance.

American Indian Medicine Wheel, the sign of the four powers of the world

Children of Judaism

If your mother were to light candles on a Friday night and the whole family were to gather together for prayers and wine and blessings, then you might be a Jewish child. Your family would be practicing the Sabbath. Sabbath means "holy day."

A mother lighting candles for the Jewish Sabbath

The name of your religion would be called Judaism. Its special sign is the Star of David. David was one of the Jewish kings. Judaism is

Jewish Star of David

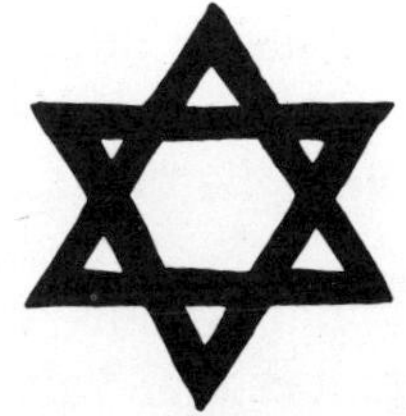

one of the oldest religions in the world. It began about 2,000 years before Jesus Christ was born. It began in the land of Ur which was part of the Middle East.

Abraham

In Ur the people thought there were gods everywhere and that the moon was the greatest god. But one man who was the chief of a large tribe of people was named Abram. Abram was beginning to think differently. When he was a very old man—99 years old—he was visited by someone who called himself the Almighty God. He and Abram had many talks together. Abram believed that this was the only true God in all the world and that the other gods were not real. God and Abram made an agreement together. Abram and his people would pray to this one God and God would choose Abram's people for his very own. He would look after them and protect them. Abram was now called Abraham by God which means "father of many people."

Yahweh

The people were supposed to keep all of God's rules and behave themselves and God would give them rewards. Some rewards were: a nice family, lots of land, plenty of food to eat. God called his new people by a new name. They were now the people of Israel and they called themselves Hebrews or Jews. Since they now believed in only one God, they taught their children this prayer: "Hear O Israel, the Lord is One." And the Jewish people called God by their own special name. It was "Yahweh."

Commandments

Yahweh made other agreements with the Jewish people. Some of these agreements became famous laws like the ones that Yahweh gave to Moses. Moses was a great leader of the Jewish people and his laws were the Ten Commandments. All of the Jewish people had to follow these laws. If you were a Jewish girl or boy, these are some of the commandments your parents would teach you:

1. Remember that Yahweh is the only God.
2. Pray to him on the Sabbath Day.
3. Obey your father and mother.
4. Do not kill, steal or lie.

5. Rest on the holy day.

These laws and stories of the Jewish people are written down in a holy book called the Torah. The Torah is not really a book like we know books. It is a long piece of paper rolled up between two sticks.

Prophets

For many years holy men would come to the Jewish people to remind them of the agreements they had made with their God, Yahweh. The holy men would tell them what might happen in the future. These men were called prophets. One of the greatest prophets was named Isaiah. He said that one day God would send a wonderful person to save the Jewish people from their sins and troubles. This person was called the Messiah.

Whenever the Jewish people are in danger or are suffering, they pray to God to send the Messiah. Christian people believe the Messiah was Jesus Christ but most Jewish people are still waiting for the Messiah to come.

Story of Esther

A very famous Jewish woman was Esther. Her people lived in the great land of King Xerxes. He chose Esther to be his queen because she was so beautiful and smart. When her people were in danger of being killed by one of the king's princes named Haman, Queen Esther very bravely went before the king to beg him to let her people live. The king loved her and granted her wish. To celebrate the courage of Esther, Jewish children have the festival of Purim. In Purim, the children dress up like Queen Esther, the king and the prince. They tell the story of how she saved the Jewish people. Special foods, breads and cookies are baked for Purim. It is a very happy holiday for Jewish children.

Jewish families who follow this old religion very carefully have strict rules and manners. Men wear small caps on the heads at all times. They put a shawl over their heads when they pray. Women dress very plainly and neatly. Jewish children are taught a certain way to wash their hands. All foods are carefully chosen, cleaned and cooked.

Mezuzah

If you go to your friends' house and you see an interesting piece of wood or metal on the door, it is probably a Jewish mezuzah. This is a very popular Jewish custom. The mezuzah might have a paper in it

Jewish mezuzah for the door post

with this prayer written on it:

> "Hear, O Israel, the Lord our God is One. You shall love the Lord your God with all your heart and your soul and your might. Put these words in your heart."

A Jewish person touches the mezuzah and says the prayer to God. If your friend meets you at the door, your friend might say "shalom" to you. This means "peace." Isn't that a nice thing to say to someone?

Bar Mitzvah

When a Jewish boy is 11 years old he starts getting ready for his Bar Mitzvah. His parents teach him to read Hebrew which is the language of his people. He might study the Torah and other books of prayers and stories. After two years, when he becomes 13 years old, he goes before the Rabbi. The Rabbi is the teacher in the Jewish church. The Jewish church is called the "synagogue." Here everyone says prayers for the boy and tells him that he is now a grown man. He is now able to teach other people about the religion of his fathers. After prayers at the synagogue, his parents have a party for him. A Jewish girl's growing-up party is called a Bat Mitzvah.

Even though the Jewish people began from a small tribe in Egypt, today there are about 14 million Jews all over the world. Jewish families live in about 65 different countries and speak different languages such as English and German and Russian. To become a Jew, you must be born in a Jewish family or else you must study the holy books and go to pray in the synagogue. The Jewish people would accept you into the Jewish religion.

Jewish boy reading the Torah

Covenant

In 1948, some of the Jewish people began to return to the land of Israel near Egypt where they started from many hundreds of years ago. Jewish people believe that this is the land that God promised them when he made his agreements with Abraham. This agreement was called the "covenant." When the Jewish people returned to Israel, they voted for men and women to be leaders and make their country strong again. They want to keep their agreement with God and live in peace and happiness.

Children of Christianity

Jesus was a Jewish boy who lived in the land of Judea. He was born almost 2,000 years ago in a stable. His mother was named Mary. She was married to a man named Joseph. Jesus always said that God in heaven was his father.

When Jesus was born, Mary and Joseph were traveling. There were no sleeping rooms left in the wayside inns. All they could find was a stable. A stable is a small barn for animals. And that is where Jesus was born. One night a great star appeared in the sky. Many people followed it. It came over the town of Bethlehem where Jesus was born. Many people believed that this was a sign from God that the

Jesus is born; a star appears

special person he promised the Jewish people had finally been born. They believed that Jesus was the person who would save them from all their troubles. They called him the Christ which means Messiah or holy person. They called themselves Christians because they believed in Jesus Christ.

Christmas

Christians celebrate Jesus' birthday on December 25th. It is called Christmas. It is a happy day when children give presents to their parents and friends. They might also receive presents. At Christmas there are traditional songs to sing and foods to eat. It is a very good time for Christians to share their love and happiness.

When Jesus was a man about 30 years old he began teaching people how to be good like his Father in heaven. He said, "You must love your parents. You should follow the Ten Commandments of the Jewish law. But more than that, you should forgive anyone who hurts you—no matter what they do to you—and no matter how many times they do it. Love everybody and love God most of all."

Miracles

Jesus worked many miracles to help people who needed something. His friends called him God's son even though he looked and acted like any other man. They said he changed water into wine at a wedding party when they were running low. He blessed a few loaves of bread and a couple of fish. They multiplied into baskets and baskets —enough to feed thousands of people. They said he made a blind person see and even brought a young man back to life after he had died. Another time he took a young girl by the hand and told her to get up. She did, and her parents were so amazed because they thought that she was lying dead on her bed. Jesus told them that she had only been sleeping. People came to him everywhere he went to hear him speak and touch him because they believed he could cure all their sickness and troubles.

Jesus especially loved poor people and little children. Whenever he traveled in the land to teach about love and forgiveness, little children came and sat on his lap. The older people tried to chase them away because they thought the children were bothering Jesus. Jesus always said, "No, let them come here with me because they are good."

When Jesus was living in Judea, his people were not free. They were ruled by the Romans. The Jewish people wanted a king who would set them free. Some people wanted Jesus to be the king. But

Jesus said that he was not a king on earth. He said that heaven was his kingdom with his Father.

Apostles

Some Jewish people were angry when Jesus talked about his Father in heaven. They didn't believe that he was the son of God. They made a plan to have him arrested and put to death. Before Jesus was arrested, he gathered his friends together. He had twelve good friends who loved him and believed in his teachings. They were called Apostles. He said to his Apostle named Simon: "I will now call you Peter because Peter means rock. A rock is strong and I need someone strong to start my church so it will last forever."

Last Supper

Jesus wanted good people to go out into the world and teach about God his Father in heaven. That night, Jesus ate a meal with his

Jesus on the cross

friends. This was called the last supper. Have you ever seen a picture of it? They shared bread and wine together. Jesus said, "This is my body and this is my blood. Eat it and drink it and remember me when I am gone."

Later Jesus was arrested and put in jail. Because he was called the son of God, some of the Jewish leaders hated him. They told the Romans that it was a great sin to think you were the son of God. For punishment, they nailed him to a cross. Jesus died. Before he died, he asked God in heaven to forgive them.

Easter

His close friends took his body down from the cross and buried it in a small grave. All the grownups and children who loved Jesus were sad, and they were crying. When they came back three days later, the grave was open and Jesus was gone. Mary Magdalene was a friend of Jesus. She was standing by the grave when someone asked her why she was crying. She said that someone had come and taken the body of Jesus away. Then she looked up and was amazed to see Jesus right in front of her. He showed her that he was alive and had risen from the dead. Christians call this time that Jesus rose Easter.

It is the most important day for Christians because they believe they will also live on with God in heaven after they die if they have obeyed God's laws. Easter is in the spring time when all new life starts again. Have you noticed how the flowers start to bloom in spring time?

Jesus came to his apostles and ate with them. He even let the Apostle Thomas touch him. They believed he was real. Then he left them. His apostles saw him go up into heaven to be with his Father.

Before he left, Jesus told his apostles that God would send his Holy Spirit to them to give them strength. The apostles said that it happened. One day they were filled with the Spirit of God and they felt strong and brave and went out into the world to tell everyone about Jesus. That is why Christians believe that there are three persons in one God: God the Father, God the Son and God the Holy Spirit. This mystery of three persons in one God is called the Trinity.

Prayer

That is how Jesus Christ's church was started. The Jewish people who believed in him now called themselves by a new name. They called themselves Christians. They came together in each other's homes to pray and share bread and wine. They said the same words Jesus did at his last supper and remembered him. Christians told the apostles and other men whom the apostles made priests the bad things that they had done. This is called confession. Then they asked the priests to forgive them and promised God to try and do better. Christian children learn this prayer that Jesus taught:

> "Our Father who is in Heaven, holy is your name. Your kingdom come, your will be done on earth as it is in heaven. Give us this day our daily bread and forgive us our trespasses, as we forgive those who trespass against us. Lead us not into temptation, but deliver us from evil."

Bible

Jesus' twelve apostles were now the leaders of his church. They traveled all over the world. They wrote down the story about the life of Jesus. They wrote down the things he said and did. They wrote letters to groups of people in other cities. Later the Christians put all these things together into a book called the New Testament. Then they put it together with the Old Testament books of the Jewish religion and made the Bible. This is the holy book of all Christians.

The Christian Bible

The Christian religion became very popular and was spreading over many countries. Missionaries went out into the world to teach about Jesus Christ. Soon the Christian church was called catholic. Catholic means "world wide." The people in this church were known as Catholics. They counted time from the day Christ was born. Any year before Christ was born was called BC which means "before Christ." AD means "after Christ." Have you noticed A.D. with a date like 1938 on the cornerstone of a building? This tells people what year the building was constructed.

Baptism

Christian parents took their tiny babies to the priest in their town. They believed their children were born with sin and wanted the sin washed away. The priest would bless some water and pour it over the children. He would pray that all sin go away from them. He would pray for God to make the children healthy and strong and keep them safe from all evil. This washing away of sin is called the sacrament of Baptism. All Christians believe Baptism is important to show God that they want to be free from all wrong and do what is right.

Today Christians have special containers of water in the churches for Baptism. There are many groups of people who believed in Jesus.

A Christian church

Even though the early Christian church was named Catholic, there are many kinds of Christian churches all over the world today. There are more chapters in this book about other Christians. Anyone from any country can become a Christian. They must believe in Jesus and be baptized.

Some names of other Christians are: Lutheran, Presbyterian, Baptist, Methodist, Episcopal, Unitarian, Mormon, Jehovah's Witness, Quaker, Mennonite, and Christian Scientist.

Cross

If you see a cross, you will know it is the special sign of Christians. It looks like the cross on which Jesus died. It reminds Christians that

Sign of the Christians

Jesus loved them so much that he would even die for them. The important thing that the Christian religion teaches us is to believe in love and forgiveness.

Children of Islam

Minaret tower of Islam

A boy kneels on a rug and bows his head until it touches the ground. He says, "Allah is Great." This is a boy of Islam. A man stands in a high tower. The tower is called a minaret. He calls out, "Allah is

Great!" He is calling the people of Islam to prayer. The people turn to their holy city five times each day and remember God. These are the people of Islam and they call their God "Allah."

Prayer

If a prayer call comes when the people are not near a church or mosque, they take out their prayer rugs and kneel on them. In Islam, all people are equal; the poor can pray together in the mosque next to the rich. Men pray together in the mosque. Sometimes women put on a special orange robe with a hood. They cover their faces with a veil. Women usually pray in their homes. The teach their children this

Moslem girl with a veil

prayer: "There is no God but Allah and Mohammed is his messenger."

A young girl in Islam learns to cook with her mother in the way the people of Islam prepare foods. They do not eat any meat from pigs. They think that pigs are not clean animals and that their meat is not fit to eat. They like to cook chicken and mutton, which is meat from sheep.

Mohammed

Islam began about 600 years after Jesus Christ was born. The person who started Islam was named Mohammed. He was a kind man.

One day he believed an angel of God came to him to visit. The angel told Mohammed that there was only one God, like the one Jewish people and Christian people worship. Before the angel came, Mohammed believed that there were many gods. But now he believed what the angel told him and wanted all the people of his country of

Arabia to believe that, too. Until then the people of Arabia believed there were many gods in the heavens and on earth. They made statues and pictures of each of the gods and said prayers to them.

Moslems

Khadija (Ha-di-ja) was Mohammed's wife. She was the first person to believe that Mohammed talked to an angel. She told Mohammed to start telling everyone about this one-God called Allah. Now Mohammed was glad that Khadija believed him and he told all of his friends and family. They started to follow him to hear more of what the angel said. They called themselves a new name because of the new way they believed in God. They called themselves Moslems. This means "one who has given himself to God."

Soon the Moslems were so many and so powerful they wanted everyone they met to think like Mohammed did. They wanted to change their country. They wanted all the Arab people to be united with God. So they began a Holy War to make people in the great city of Mecca listen to them. The Moslems did not think war was wrong. They thought it was the only way to make people listen to them. They were strong. They marched into Mecca and broke the statues of other gods. The people in Mecca listened to Mohammed and began to believe in Allah. They called their new religion Islam.

Koran

If you were a Moslem child, you would probably learn to read and speak Arabic. You might read in a large book called the Koran. The Koran is the holy book of Islam. Moslems believe that all the words the

Koran, the holy book of Islam

angel of God spoke to Mohammed are in this holy book.

All Moslem children learn five duties:

1. Say this prayer: "There is no God but Allah, and Mohammed is his messenger."
2. Pray five times each day.
3. Only eat and drink Islam's special foods on fast days.
4. Make a trip to the Holy City of Mecca at least once in your life.
5. Give help to the poor and hungry people.

Moslems call themselves brothers of the Jews and Christians. They think that Abraham and Moses and Jesus were holy men. But Moslems believe that Mohammed is the last and greatest of the holy men. They think that each person can speak to God without the help of a priest or rabbi or teacher. Some Moslems also believe it is good to have more than one wife as long as each wife is treated equally.

Mecca

The greatest holiday of the Moslems is called Hajj. It is when someone takes a trip to the city of Mecca in Arabia. Sometimes a whole family takes the trip together. The men wear white pants and shirts and the women wear long simple dresses. All the people dress alike to show that they are equal in the eyes of God. Moslems take the trip to Mecca to pray at the Black Stone. The stone was very special to the Arab people even before Mohammed lived. They believed it fell from heaven. Mohammed told the people of Mecca that the stone was a gift from Allah and that the people could come to it when they prayed to Allah. Sometimes they kiss the stone or just touch it.

Once Mohammed was the only person in Arabia who believed in Allah. Now many, many people in the world are Moslems, over 500 million. Who can be a Moslem? Any person in any country can become a Moslem if they believe in the teachings of Mohammed. If you see a sign with the half moon and the star, you will know that it means the people of Islam.

An important thing that the Islam religion teaches us is that there is nothing and no one more important than God. Children of Islam do not have pictures or statues of God, but they learn to think of him every day at prayer time.

Children of Catholic and Eastern Orthodox Religions

Catholics were the first Christians. Their leaders were called bishops and priests. Young men become priests by studying the Bible and the teachings of the Catholic Church. When a bishop touches his hands on a young man's head he becomes a priest. The new priest then has the right to say the Mass, baptize babies, and forgive people their sins. Only men are allowed to be priests in the Catholic Church.

Bishops and priests and all Catholics have a leader. He is called the Pope or the Holy Father. The Pope lives in Rome, Italy. His people are called Roman Catholics. There are about 550 million Roman Catholics in the world today.

Doctrines

Boys and girls in the Roman Catholic Church study the teachings of the holy book called the Bible. They also study the teachings of the Church. These teachings are called doctrines. Catholics believe that the doctrines the Pope teaches are the true words of God. They believe the Pope is close to God and that God helps him make correct decisions.

Here are some things that Catholics teach their children:

1. There is only one God, but there are three persons in one God.
2. God is perfect. He is everywhere. He never began and he will never end.
3. God made the world, the sun, moon, stars, men and women, animals and angels.
4. Jesus is God's son.

The special sign of Catholics is the cross with Jesus nailed on it. It reminds them that Jesus loved them so much, he even died for them. It is called a crucifix.

Catholic children believe they have a good angel that watches over them. An angel is a spirit that God made. They also believe that there are bad angels that turned away from God. The bad angels try to get people to turn away from God, too. Disobeying God is called sin.

Catholic parents take their tiny babies to the priest for Baptism just like the early Christians did. Catholics can go to church and pray any time they want too. But they must go to church on Sunday. That is their holy day.

First Communion

When boys and girls are about seven years old, they come to the center of the church to receive their first communion. Sometimes they dress in white to show that they are good. At the church, special prayers are said. This is called "Mass." During Mass, the priest blesses bread and wine. The bread is on a golden plate and the wine is in a golden cup. The priest says the words that Jesus said at his last supper.

Bread and wine at the Mass

All the Catholics believe that the bread and wine really become the body and blood of Jesus. Even though it looks like bread and wine, they believe it changes. The children and the parents then take the bread and eat it. This is called communion. It means "sharing." They believe that now Jesus is in them.

Prayers

Have you ever seen your friends touch their head, heart and both shoulders before eating a meal? They are saying a thank you prayer to God and making the sign of the cross. It reminds them of the Father, Son and Holy Spirit.

Priest making the sign of the cross

If you are in your friend's home, you might see a rosary. It is a string of beads with a cross on the end. The rosary is used to count prayers. The prayers are to God the Father and to Mary, the mother of Jesus. Catholics often ask Mary to help them because she was so close to Jesus and his Father in heaven. You may see a statue of Mary with a candle in front of it in your friend's home.

Each year many Catholics go to church on Ash Wednesday. It comes in the spring, 40 days before Easter. The priest puts a dot of ashes on people's foreheads. This is how they remember that their bodies will turn to dusty ashes when they die, but their souls will live on forever with Jesus in heaven.

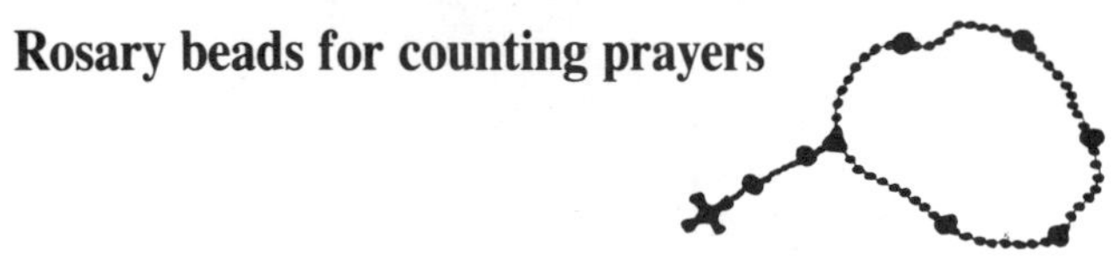

Rosary beads for counting prayers

Orthodox

Another church that is very much like the Roman Catholic Church is called Orthodox. That is two Greek words put together. Ortho means "true." Doxa means "idea." True idea.

How did this church start? You remember that after Jesus died and went to heaven, his twelve apostles went all over the world. Apostle Andrew went to Russia and Apostle Paul went to Greece. The Russian and Greek people believed everything that Andrew and Paul taught them about Jesus. They wrote many books and started many schools to teach about the life of Jesus. They built beautiful churches. The churches in Russia are almost always white because white means pure and good. A gold dome is at the top of the steeple. It looks like a big onion-shaped crown. The inside walls are filled with paintings of Jesus and the great things he did in his life. The paintings are watercolors that were put on wet plaster walls. They are called frescos.

Monks and Nuns

Some men and women in this church did not want to earn money or be powerful or get married. They only wanted to study about God and pray for themselves and the world. They started schools called

Orthodox church

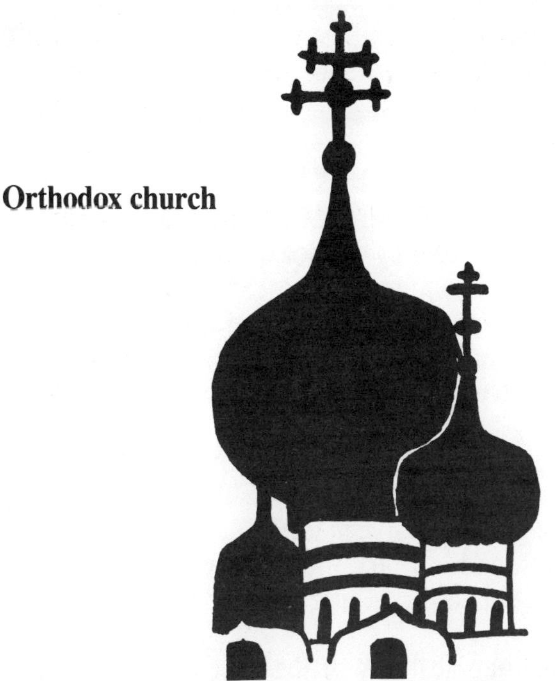

monasteries. The men that joined the monasteries were called brothers or monks. The Roman Catholic Church also has monks. Women who want to do this live together in houses called convents. They are called sisters or nuns.

Monks were happy feeling close to God. They wrote new prayers and songs to sing in church. Other monks painted pictures of Jesus. These are icons. Icons are beautiful. They are made of wood or metal and they come in all sizes. You might find a little one in the home of an Orthodox friend. Families light candles in front of the icon and kiss it to show how much they love Jesus. The bigger icons are set alongside

An icon of Jesus

the road. On certain days, families walk to these places with oil lamps and candles. The icons help them feel safe and protected on their trip.

Council

Orthodox people were part of the Catholic Church until the year 1054. Then they decided they did not want to obey the Pope in Rome. They didn't believe one man could make important decisions all by himself. They thought that a group of people should make the decisions. They called this group the "Council." They believed the council had the true idea. This is why they called themselves "Orthodox."

Even though they did not agree about the Pope, people in the Orthodox church still believe most of the same teachings as the Roman Catholics. They believe in the Bible, the real body and blood of Jesus in the Mass, and in Mary, the mother of Jesus. They believe in their religion as easily as breathing in and out. It is in their lives every day.

Easter is the happiest day of the year for the Orthodox people. They are happy that Jesus rose from the dead. People bring Easter eggs and cake and Easter bread to the church. The priest blesses the food and gives each person some Easter bread to eat. The bread is tall and round and decorated.

Easter bread

Pentecost

Seven Sundays after Easter is Pentecost. This was the time when the apostles felt the Spirit of God come to them after Jesus left. To remember the day when the apostles were filled with the Holy Spirit of God, the priest holds candles high above his head. In one hand he holds two candles to show that Jesus was both God and man. In the other hand the priest holds three candles to show the three persons in one God.

Priest with candle sticks for Pentecost

When Eastern Orthodox children are in church they do not play guitars or organs or pianos. But they do sing songs to God with their voices. If they are sick and can't get to church, the priest will come to visit them. The priest will also come to each person's home for something important like planting new crops in the fields or getting the boats ready for the fishing season.

A sign that is often used in the Orthodox church is a cross with the letter "P." It is called the Chi Rho (sounds like "key row"). It is the sign of Jesus.

Sign of the Orthodox Church, the Chi Rho

Eastern Orthodox boys and girls have birthdays like everyone else. Much more important though, is that they celebrate their name day. When they are born, their parents give them the name of a holy person who was part of their church. This holy person is called a "saint." If you were named Andrew, your family would give you a party and presents on Saint Andrew's special day. Now can you see how important religion is to an Orthodox family?

Children of Protestant Religions

About 500 years ago many people stopped believing in some of the rules and teachings of the Catholic Church. Remember, back then the Catholic Church was in many countries in the world and the Pope in Rome was its leader. Some people said they did not agree with the Pope or the rules of the Church and they made a protest. These people were called by a new name—"Protestant," or "Evangelical." Evangelical means agreeing with the New Testament books of the Bible.

Martin Luther

Protestants were Christians because they believed that Jesus was the Son of God. But they were no longer Catholic Christians. One of the first protests started with a man named Martin Luther. He was a Roman Catholic boy. Something happened to him one day when he was out for a walk. He was struck by lightning. A bolt of lightning hit

Martin Luther being struck by lightning

him but he did not die. He was very scared and frightened, though, because he knew that he could have died right there on the spot. That started him thinking about what would happen if he died and left this earth. What would God say to him? Would God judge him good or bad? Would he go to heaven or hell? Christians believe that a person goes to hell after they die only if they are very bad.

Martin Luther really wanted to be good. He joined a monastery and became a monk. He did hard work. He prayed. He fasted often and did not eat much food. He studied the rules of the Catholic church. There were some rules that he did not like. He started thinking his own thoughts.

Faith

Martin Luther was sure that God would judge people when they died. He was sure that God would punish people if they were bad. But he thought if people believed in Jesus they would be safe from punishment. He said, "People must have faith in God and his son, Jesus."

Do you know what faith is? It is hard to understand. To have faith means to be sure of something even if you cannot see it or touch it or hear it. When you go to bed tonight in the dark, you are sure that the sun will shine again in the morning. You cannot see the sunshine tonight, but you believe it will be there tomorrow. That's what faith is.

This belief or faith in God was the only thing that Martin Luther thought was important. He said, "Faith is how you get to heaven when you die, not be obeying all the rules of a church."

So it happened that Martin Luther started his protest. He did not agree that the Pope was always right about everything in the church. He thought that the Pope was just like any other person, and could make mistakes about the church's teachings. Then Martin Luther talked about the priests and monks. He did not believe that they were holier or more special to God just because they were priests. He thought they were just like other people, and that they should be allowed to get married and have families. He said the Church should not tell people how to live—people would know the right way to live just by learning the words of the Bible.

Printing Press

This was a very important idea but many people at that time could not read. There weren't very many books. The priests and monks could read though, and they told the people what the books said and what they meant.

Now just about the time that Martin Luther started his disagreement with the Catholic Church, a new machine was invented. This invention was called a printing press. It could make books fast that

A printing press

were easy to read. Martin Luther had his ideas printed in books on the new printing press in Germany. People started to learn to read more easily now.

The books that Martin Luther wrote were sent to many countries, and many people read them. Some people agreed with the ideas of Martin Luther. But his ideas also upset a lot of people in the Catholic Church. This Church had been the main religion of all these countries for over 1500 years. They did not want it changed. The Pope told Martin Luther to stop his ideas and apologize.

Martin Luther said, "I think I am right. I will not apologize." Then the Pope told him that he could not be a Catholic any more. Martin Luther said, "All right." He took his own ideas and wrote more books and started his own church. The people that left the Catholic Church and joined Martin Luther were called Evangelicals.

New Churches

So the first Protestant Church was the Lutheran or Evangelical Church which started about the year 1520. Other friends of Martin Luther went back to their own countries and started their own protests. New churches started all over Europe. These new churches soon came to America. America was unusual because people had the freedom to believe in any religion they wanted to. Today in the Lutheran church both men and women are leaders and ministers.

After Martin Luther left, the Roman Catholic Church did change some of its rules. But many people had already left the church. The two ideas that both Catholics and Protestants agree on are: Baptism washes away sins, and communion of bread and wine shares the love that Jesus showed his people at the last supper.

Still there is a difference. Catholics believe the bread and wine really and truly become the body of Jesus, and Protestants believe it is just a nice way to remember that Jesus loved them so much that he died for them. He gave up his body and blood for them.

If you were a Protestant child, you would study the Bible and learn about God's love and his son, Jesus Christ. You would say the prayer that Jesus taught—"Our Father who is in Heaven."

Other Protestant religions besides Lutherans are:

Methodists

Methodists were started by John and Charles Wesley. They believed that teaching and singing were important at church. They also thought that every boy and girl had a free will. That means that you can choose between right things and wrong things yourself.

Anglicans or Episcopalians

These churches started in England. These churches are very much like the Catholic Church. They also think that lessons and singing songs to God during worship service are very important. Women can be leaders in this church in America.

Baptists

Baptist churches started in England also, but they are most popular in the United States today. Many Baptist churches believe in sending missionaries to other countries to teach people about their religion. There are many kinds of Baptist churches, but all of them believe the words of the Bible are from God. Baptist boys and girls learn to say parts of the Bible by heart.

If you were a tiny baby in the Baptist religion, your parents wouldn't take you to the church to be baptized. They would let you wait until you were old enough to understand about Jesus yourself. You would believe that Jesus was sent to save you. If you decided to accept Jesus as your personal savior, then the minister in your church would baptize you by dunking you totally under the water to wash away your sins.

Christian Baptism

Christian Scientists

This is a church that started in America in the year 1879. It was started by a woman named Mary Baker Eddy. She believed everything that was wrong with the world could be made better. All sins and sickness and bad things could be taken away by healing. She remembered the stories of Jesus when he would touch people and make them better. Mary Baker Eddy thought that anybody could do this also if he or she believed in Jesus the Healer. Christian Scientist children do not always take medicines or have operations for sicknesses. Their parents feel they can get better by touching the children and praying to Jesus.

Working for Peace

There are many other kinds of churches, too. The most important thing to remember is that each Protestant religion is Christian. Each religion makes its own rules and has its own leaders. Christians are not all united like they were when the Pope was their leader. They do not call the Pope Holy Father like Catholics do. But Christians today are now working together. They know they are all children of God living together on earth. They are working for peace in the world. Someday you might want to work for peace, too. This is one sign for peace.

The modern sign of peace

Children of the Church of Jesus Christ of Latter-Day Saints (Mormons)

"Mormon" is a nickname for someone who belongs to the Church of Jesus Christ of Latter-Day Saints. Mormons are Christians because they believe that Jesus is God's Son and that the Virgin Mary was his mother. But they are not Protestant or Catholic.

Joseph Smith

This church was started in 1830 by a boy named Joseph Smith. He was about 15 years old. He went out into his father's fields one day to pray. He felt something unusual had happened to him. He went back home and told his family:

> "Suddenly God appeared to me. He told me to bring back the teachings of Jesus. Many people have forgotten about the Bible."

Joseph lived in New York at the time. Soon many people began to believe in his ideas. Joseph Smith said an angel came to him one day and showed him some golden plates. On the plates were written messages. The messages told about histories of people in Asia and America. Joseph Smith wrote this idea down in the Book of Mormon. So the holy books in the Mormon Church are the Bible and the Book of Mormon. The angel that came to him told him to start a new church.

Beehive, Mormon sign of hard work

Pioneers

The followers of the Mormon Church were some of the first pioneers. They kept moving West from New York into Ohio, Missouri, Illinois and finally they came to Utah. There they built a beautiful

Mormons' travel across America

temple. There are many small Mormon churches called chapels everywhere where anyone can come and pray. But only Mormons can go into a temple. Temples are used for weddings and funerals. There are about 16 temples in the world.

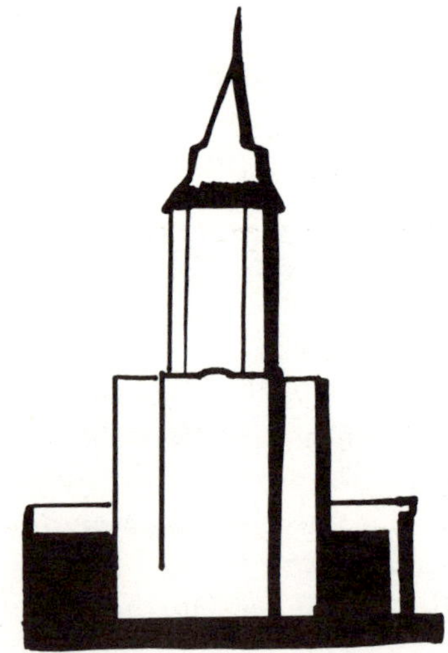

A Mormon temple

Mormon children come into the Church when they are about eight years old. They also have the special ceremony called Baptism when they are dunked into a tub of water to wash away their sins.

Water is a sign of being clean. They share bread and water to remember Jesus at the last supper. But they don't believe that the bread and water really change into the body and blood of Jesus.

Missionaries

Anyone is allowed to join the Mormon Church, but women cannot be leaders in the Mormon Church. Girls, women and older couples are allowed to go out for a short time and tell people about the Mormon Church. They are called missionaries.

Have you ever seen two young men dressed in black suits walking around your neighborhood carrying the Bible? These might be young Mormon men. They are priests of their church for about two years. They go to each door and answer questions about their religion. These men don't get paid for their work as priests so they usually keep their regular jobs also. Mormon women usually do not wear jewelry, and they dress very simply. One of the rules of this church is: "You must not smoke tobacco or drink hard drinks that will injure your health." That is why Mormons believe they are some of the healthiest people in the world.

Mormon parents teach their children that we ALL will go to heaven when we die and be with our family and friends. But some of us will be happier there than others. It depends on how good we have been and how much we have learned. This is why Mormon parents believe it is very important for boys and girls to go to school and get a good education. If you were a Mormon child, your family would often set aside a night just for family things like talking and playing and learning about God's love. Mormon children are expected to work very hard. Their parents show them that this can be fun, too. They show them that after hard work come many rewards. One important thing the Mormon Church teaches us is to take care of widows who have lost their husbands. They also take care of children who have no parents. A good Mormon family will take orphan children right into their own home and love them like their own children.

Even though Mormons have traveled to different countries, you will find many Mormons near Salt Lake City, Utah, where they have a very famous group of singers called the Mormon Tabernacle Choir.

Epilogue

Did you find your religion in this book? Do you know which ones your friends belong to? Isn't it nice to know that so many people can live together even though they believe different things? It really isn't hard at all if we respect everyone.

God has many children who believe different teachings, and each one of us is loved. We can be happy in this love and show it to others by living in peace with everyone. Just think, there are not even two snowflakes alike! Yet all the snow lies together on the earth in peace. People everywhere can live in peace together too. There is room for everyone.

"Little children, you are of God." (I John 4:4), and we wish *you* peace.

Sincerely,

Dr. Thomas
Mrs. Ramey

Glossary and Index

angel	p. 39	*(ain jel) a being made by God, a spirit messenger from God
Apostles	p. 32	(a po sels) twelve people chosen by Jesus Christ to take his teachings into the world
Aryans	p. 6	(air ee ans) light-skinned people from Europe or Asia
Baptism	p. 35	(bap tiz em) sprinkling with water or dunking under water, a sacrament in Christian religions
Bar Mitzvah	p. 28	(bar mitz vah) ceremony for a Jewish boy's 13th birthday
Bat Mitzvah	p. 28	(bat mits vah) ceremony for a Jewish girl's 13th birthday
black stone	p. 40	holy stone of the Islamic faith in Mecca
Brahma	p. 10	(bra ma) Supreme being of the Hindu religion who has three beings in one: Brahma, Vishnu and Shiva
Buddha	p. 14	(boo da) Siddhartha Gautama, founder of Buddhism, means "enlightened one"
Buddhism	p. 13	(boo dism) religion of Asia that teaches self-denial and middle way
caste	p. 6	(kast) Hindu class of people
Catholic	p. 41	(kath o lik) a Christian Church, usually means Roman Catholic, founded by Jesus Christ and continued by the apostles
Christian	p. 30	(kris chun) a person who believes in the teachings and life of Jesus Christ
Christian Science	p. 54	religion that teaches that human suffering can be removed by faith in Jesus Christ, prayer and curing by touching; founded by Mary Baker Eddy
Christmas	p. 31	(kris mus) Christian holiday that celebrates the birth of Jesus Christ
communion	p. 42	(kum you nyon) eating bread and wine that is blessed to remember the last supper of Jesus Christ
confession	p. 34	(kon fe shun) telling what you did wrong, being sorry for it, and promising not to do it again

* *Words in parentheses are phonetic speech sounds.*

covenant	p. 29	(kuv e nent) an agreement between God and Abraham
Divali	p. 9	(dee va lee) Hindu celebration for the end of old year and beginning of new year
dome	p. 44	(dohm) a round roof on top of a building or church
Easter	p. 33	(ees ter) a special springtime celebration of the Christian Church which remembers Christ's death and rising from the dead
Egyptian religion	p. 1	(e jip shun) beliefs of the people of Egypt in Northern Africa in ancient times
Esther	p. 27	(es ter) a Jewish Queen who saved her people from death
faith	p. 50	(fayth) believing in something without proof, believing in a Supreme Being without actually seeing him
fasting	p. 19	choosing not to eat food for a day or more
Ganges	p. 11	(gang ees) a holy river in the Hindu religion in India
God	p. 10	a name given to the Supreme Being
god	p. 10	any male being believed to be divine with power over human beings
goddess	p. 3	(god is) any female being believed to be divine with power over humans
Hajj	p. 40	a holy trip to Mecca in Saudi Arabia, a rule of the Islamic faith
heaven	p. 30	(hev en) a place of reward for souls of good people after they die on this earth
hell	p. 50	a place of punishment for souls of bad people after they die on this earth
Hindu	p. 6	(hin du) a East Indian person in language and religion
icon	p. 45	(eye con) a holy picture usually of Jesus Christ in the Eastern Orthodox Church
Islam	p. 37	(is lahm) the religion of the people of Mohammed, also called Moslems
Jesus Christ	p. 30	a Jewish person said to be the son of God and the person promised to save the Jewish people. He started the religion that is now called Christian.

Judaism	p. 25	(jew dae ism) religion of the Jewish people founded by Abraham
karma	p. 9	(kar ma) reward for being good and punishment for being bad until one is good enough to leave the wheel of life and go on to the Hindu place of happiness called nirvana
Koran	p. 39	(kor an) the holy book of the Islam religion
lamas	p. 15	(lah mas) priests or monks in the Buddhist religion in Tibet
lotus	p. 17	(low tus) a water lily, also a sign of the Buddhist religion
Lutheran	p. 52	Protestant church begun by Martin Luther in 1520
Martin Luther	p. 49	a monk in the Catholic Church who disagreed with some of the rules of the church and started his own religion
Mass	p. 42	a church service in the Catholic and Episcopalian churches that remembers the last supper and death of Jesus Christ
Mecca	p. 40	(mek ka) the holy city of Islam religion in Saudi Arabia
meditation	p. 15	(med i ta shun) thinking quietly and deeply of only one thing, keeping your mind silent to hear God speak to you
mezuzah	p. 28	(me zu za) a piece of wood or metal with a Jewish prayer
missionary	p. 53	(mis shun air ee) a person who travels in the world and teaches other people about his religion
Mohammed	p. 38	(mo ha med) the founder of the Islam religion
monastery	p. 45	(mon a stair ee) building where monks live away from the rest of the world
monk	p. 45	(munk) a man who lives away from the rest of the world and gives his life only to his God
Moslem	p. 39	(mus lem) a person who follows the Islam religion of Mohammed
Muslim	p. 39	(mus lem) another name for a person who follows the religion of Mohammed
mummy	p. 4	(mum ee) a human body cleaned and wrapped to be buried, Egyptian method of burial

myths	p. 1	(miths) stories about peoples and gods that cannot be proven true
Nile River	p. 1	a huge river in the land of Egypt
nirvana	p. 9	(nir va na) a place where there is eternal peace with no worries or pain
nun	p. 16	(none) a woman who gives her whole life to her God
Orthodox Church	p. 44	(or tho docks) a Christian Church in eastern Europe that broke away from the Catholic Church
Pentecost	p. 47	(pen ta cost) the day Christian people celebrate the coming of the Holy Spirit
pharaoh	p. 3	(fair oh) the name of the kings of ancient Egypt
Pope	p. 41	leader of the Roman Catholic Church and Bishop of Rome. He is sometimes called Holy Father
prophet	p. 27	(prah fet) a person who tells what will happen in the future . . . a messenger that God sends to his people
Protestant	p. 49	(prah tes tent) a person in a Christian church that is not Roman Catholic or Orthodox or Mormon
Purim	p. 27	(poo rem) a holiday in the Jewish religion that celebrates the brave Queen Esther
pyramid	p. 3	(pir a mid) a building that is made of triangles that come together in a point at the top. Egyptian kings were buried in them.
rabbi	p. 28	(ra bye) a teacher of Jewish holy books and laws in the Jewish religion
reincarnation	p. 8	(re in car na shun) being born again into a new body after a person dies
religion	p. 1	(re li jun) a belief in a divine power who created the world and who should be obeyed and worshipped
rosary	p. 43	(rose a ree) a string of beads used in counting prayers
Sabbath	p. 25	(sa beth) a day of rest and prayer in the Jewish religion
sacrament	p. 35	a sign or symbol in the Christian Church
sacrifice	p. 2	(sa cri fice) giving up something that you really want to keep for yourself
saint	p. 48	a holy person in a Christian church

sari	p. 9	(sah ree) a long piece of silk or cotton worn by Hindu women as traditional dress
Sequoia	p. 20	(see kuoy ya) a Cherokee Chief who wrote down the first Indian language so that it could be easily understood
shaman	p. 22	(shah man) the medicine man of an American Indian tribe. He is both their doctor and priest
Siddhartha	p. 13	(sid har tha) Siddhartha Gautama was the founder of the Buddhist religion
sin	p. 42	deciding not to obey the law of God
Sun Dance	p. 19	an American Indian holiday of prayer, fasting, and dancing
synagogue	p. 29	(sin a gog) a building where the Jewish people come together for prayer
Ten Commandments	p. 26	ten laws that were given to Moses, a leader of the Jewish people, by God
Torah	p. 27	(tor ah) the first five books of the Jewish holy books. It is a scroll rolled up between two sticks.
tradition	p. 20	(trah di shun) telling a story over and over again to your children and grandchildren
trespass	p. 34	(tress pass) sin
trinity	p. 33	(trin i tee) the idea that there are three persons in one God
untouchables	p. 7	the lowest group of people in old Hindu society who had to do the worst jobs
Vedas	p. 9	(vay das) the holy book of the Hindu religion and the oldest known religious writings on earth
Vedism	p. 6	(vay dism) one of the oldest religions in India that say there are many gods
vision	p. 22	(vi shun) a dream or idea that comes from the spirit world in the American Indian religion
wayside inn	p. 30	a small hotel where travellers could eat and sleep overnight
Wheel of Life	p. 8	the Hindu circle of life, death, and rebirth
yoga	p. 11	(yoh gah) exercise to relax and control the mind and the body. It is sometimes used to teach meditation.
Zen	p. 18	a kind of Buddhist religion that uses meditation to look inside yourself for the truth

Bibliography

Berger, Gilda, *Religion: A First Reference Book*, Franklin Watts, New York, New York, 1983.

Blackman, Milton V. Jr., *Christian Churches of America: Origins and Beliefs*, revised edition, Chas. Scribner's Sons, New York, NY, 1983.

Capps, Walter H., *Seeing With a Native Eye*, Harper & Row, New York, NY, 1976.

Cone, Molly, *Purim*, Thomas Y. Crowell Co., New York, NY, 1967.

Edmonds, I.G., *Buddhism*, Franklin Watts, New York, NY, 1978.

Edmonds, I.G., *Islam*, Franklin Watts, New York, NY, 1977.

Edmonds, I.G., *Other Lives: The Story of Reincarnation*, McGraw Hill Book Co., New York, NY, 1979.

Elgin, Kathleen, *The Mormons,* David McKay Co., Inc., New York, NY, 1969.

Fitch, Florence M., *Allah, The God of Islam*, Lothrop, Lee & Shepard Co., Inc., New York, NY, 1962.

Gage, Nicholas, *Portrait of Greece*, American Heritage Press, New York, NY, 1971.

Harrer, Heinrich, *Seven Years in Tibet*, E.P. Dutton & Co., New York, NY, 1954.

Haskins, James, *Religions,* J.B. Lippincott Co., Philadelphia, PA, 1973.

Ions, Veronica, *Indian Mythology*, Hamlyn Publishing Co., London, England, 1968.

Ions, Veronica, *Egyptian Mythology*, Peter Bedrick Books, New York, NY, 1982.

Ingrams, Doreen, *Mosques and Minarets*, EMC Corporation, St. Paul, MN, 1974.

Kettlekamp, Larry, *Religions East and West*, Wm. Morrow & Co., New York, NY, 1972.

Kleeberg, Irene Cumming, *Christianity*, Franklin Watts, New York, NY, 1976.

Lach, Samuel T. & Wachs, Saul R., *Judaism*, Donald K. Swearer, ed., Argue Communication, Niles, IL, 1979.

Latourette, Kenneth, *A History of Christianity, Vol. II.*, revised edition, Harper & Row Publishers, New York, NY, 1975.

Liston, Robert A., *By These Faiths—Religions for Today*, Julian Messner, New York, NY, 1977.

Henry R. Luce et. al., eds., *The World's Greatest Religions,* Western Publishing Co., 1972.

Marriott, Alice & Rachlin, Carol K., *Plains Indian Mythology*, Thomas Y. Crowell Co., New York, NY, 1975.

Pardue, Peter A., *Buddhism*, MacMillan Co., New York, NY, 1971.

Pfeifer, Charles F., *The Dead Sea Scrolls and the Bible*, Baker Book House Co., New York, NY, 1969.

Archbishop Pitirim of Volokolamus, ed., *The Orthodox Church in Russia*, The Vwndome Press, New York, NY, 1982.

Chas. S. Prebish, ed., *Buddhism: A Modern Prospectus*, Penn. State University Park Press, University Park, PA, 1975.

Rice, Edward, *The Five Great Religions*, Four Winds Press, New York, NY, 1973.

Rice, Edward, *Ten Religions of the East*, Four Winds Press, New York, NY, 1978.

Ross, Nancy W., *Buddhism: A Way of Life and Thought*, Alfred A. Knopf, New York, NY, 1980.

Leo Rosteb, ed., *Religions of America*, Simon & Schuster, New York, NY, 1975.

Starkloff, Carl, *The People of the Center*, The Seabury Press, New York, NY, 1974.

Tedlock, Barbara & Dennis, *Teachings from the American Earth*, Liveright, New York, NY, 1975.

The Mormons, Church of Jesus Christ of Latter-Day Saints, Deseret Book Company, 1978.

MANY CHILDREN STUDY GUIDE MASTERS

for your classroom

These Study Guide Masters are excellent additions to **Many Children**'s chapters and are suitable for copying. They include chapter sheets of activities, discussion questions, additional reading suggestions, an inclusive test and teacher answer sheet and a certificate of achievement. Learning level: Third through sixth grade. Allow 4-6 weeks for delivery.

Please send me ________ **Many Children Study Guide** set(s) at $3.00 each including postage and handling. My check or money order is enclosed for $ ____________.

MANY CHILDREN STUDY GUIDES
2055 Royal Fern Court 21B, Reston, VA 22091

Name ______________________________________ Phone ____________

Address ____

City ________________________________ State _____ ZIP ________

VOLUME DISCOUNTS

The following discounts are available for volume orders of **Many Children—Religions Around The World,** first edition. Single copy price is $6.95 plus $1.75 for postage and handling. Allow 4-6 weeks for delivery.

Copies	Discount	Discounted Price Each	Total Postage and Handling
10-19	10%	$6.25	$3.00
20-29	15%	$5.90	$3.75
30-40	20%	$5.55	$4.50

Please send me _____ copies of **Many Children—Religions Around The World** at $________ each for a total of $____________ plus $________ for postage and handling. My check or money order is enclosed for $___________.

MANY CHILDREN DISCOUNTS
2055 Royal Fern Court 21B, Reston, VA 22091

Name ______________________________________ Phone ____________

Address ____

City ________________________________ State _____ ZIP ________

MANY CHILDREN COLORING BOOKS

This PRIMARY level edition of **Many Children—Religions Around The World** introduces younger readers to friends, cultures and religions of the world. Learning level: Preschool through second grade in a take-me-home coloring book format (24 pages). Available in March 1988. Allow 4-6 weeks for delivery.

Please send me ________ **Many Children Coloring Book**(s) at $1.50 each including postage and handling. My check or money order is enclosed for $ ____________.

MANY CHILDREN COLORING BOOKS
2055 Royal Fern Court 21B, Reston, VA 22091

Name ______________________________________ Phone ____________

Address ____

City ________________________________ State _____ ZIP ________

Take advantage of
these handy coupons.

Cut out and mail today.